STRANGE SCIENCE

HOW DO X-RAYS SOLVE MYSTERIES?

BY ANNA CLAYBOURNE
AND TIM WESSON

Gareth Stevens
PUBLISHING

Please visit our website, www.garethstevens.com. For a free color catalog of all our high-quality books, call toll free 1-800-542-2595 or fax 1-877-542-2596.

Cataloging-in-Publication Data
Names: Claybourne, Anna. | Wesson, Tim.
Title: How do x-rays solve mysteries? / by Anna Claybourne and Tim Wesson.
Description: Buffalo, NY : Gareth Stevens Publishing, 2027. | Series: Strange science | Includes glossary and index.
Identifiers: ISBN 9781482478341 (pbk.) | ISBN 9781482478358 (library bound) | ISBN 9781482478365 (ebook)
Subjects: LCSH: Machinery--Juvenile literature. | Machinery--Miscellanea--Juvenile literature.
Classification: LCC TJ147.C53 2027 | DDC 621.8--dc23

Published in 2027 by
Gareth Stevens Publishing
2544 Clinton St.
Buffalo, NY 14224

First published in Great Britain in 2025 by wayland

Commissioning editor: Melanie Palmer
Designer: Lisa Peacock

Printed in China
CPSIA compliance information: Batch #QS27GS: For further information contact Gareth Stevens at 1-800-542-2595.

CONTENTS

THE SILLY SCIENCE OF MACHINES

Hi there!
It's me, Professor Splat...
along with a few of
my favorite machines!

Whhoooaa ...
how do you steer
this thing?

MARVELOUS MACHINES

FOR THOUSANDS OF YEARS, HUMANS HAVE BEEN MAKING ALL KINDS OF MACHINES TO MAKE LIFE EASIER – FROM THE FIRST WHEELS TO FLUSHING TOILETS, FLYING CARS, AND COMPUTER TECHNOLOGY!

SNIP!
SNIP!

MACHINES DON'T HAVE TO BE HIGH-TECH. THEY CAN BE SMALL AND SIMPLE, LIKE A PAIR OF SCISSORS.

Like me!

BUT THESE DAYS WE HAVE ALL KINDS OF AMAZING SUPER-ADVANCED MACHINES TOO.

DID YOU KNOW THAT ...

• Some planes have no engine – just pedals ...

Look out!

• We've built dozens of different kinds of robot animals ...

From flies and bees ...

... to chimpanzees!

• There are even machines so small you can't see them!

Is anyhting here?
No idea!

You're about to find out!

SO MANY QUESTIONS!

WHO WAS THE FIRST TO THINK OF WHEELS?
HOW CAN YOU LAUNCH YOURSELF OVER A CASTLE WALL?
WHAT DO TALKING TOILETS SAY?
HOW DOES A GPS KNOW THE WAY?
AND HOW DID THE COMPUTER MOUSE GET ITS NAME?

WONDERFUL WHEELS

ABOUT 6,000 YEARS AGO, IN ANCIENT MESOPOTAMIA ... MOVING BIG STONES WAS A BIG HASSLE!
Roll it along!
Now stop!
THEN ...
Bring those logs round to the front!
LARGE OBJECTS WERE ROLLED ON LOGS – BUT YOU HAD TO KEEP MOVING THE LOGS!
SO ...
Does that work any better?
THEY TRIED PULLING THE STONES ON SLEDS INSTEAD
AND ...
What if we put the sled ON the logs?

Ooh look! The sled is starting to wear grooves in the logs.
Hey – I've got an idea!
If we cut this part away, the logs will be lighter and easier to move.
Putting pegs here will hold the log in one place, so it spins round and doesn't roll away.
THE LOGS HAVE BECOME TWO WHEELS ON AN AXLE ...
We don't need to carve logs – we can just make wheels and stick them on a pole! Brilliant!
WHEELED CARTS HAVE ARRIVED!
FINALLY ...
This isn't fair! Lazy humans!

KEEP ON ROLLING...

NO ONE KNOWS EXACTLY WHERE AND WHEN THE WHEEL WAS INVENTED – BUT WE THINK THIS IS PROBABLY HOW IT HAPPENED.

And it became one of the most important machines of all time!

WHEELS EVERYWHERE!

WHEELS AREN'T JUST FOR TRANSPORTATION. THE SAME IDEA IS USED IN ALL KINDS OF OTHER MACHINES TOO...

COGS AND GEARS

WINDMILL

RECORD PLAYER

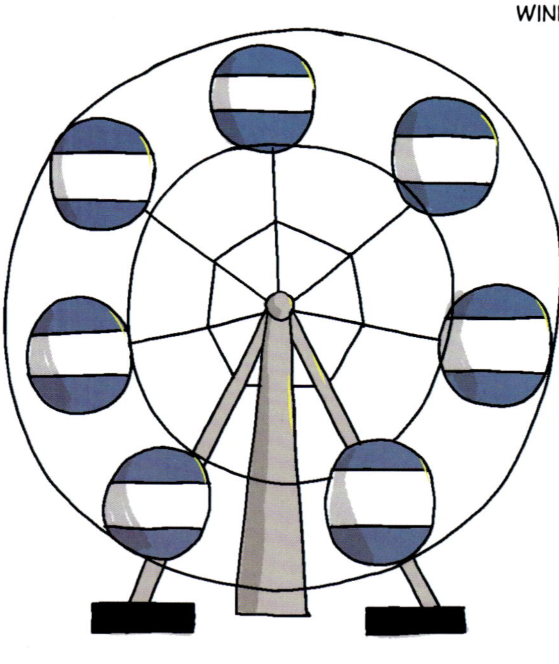
FERRIS WHEEL

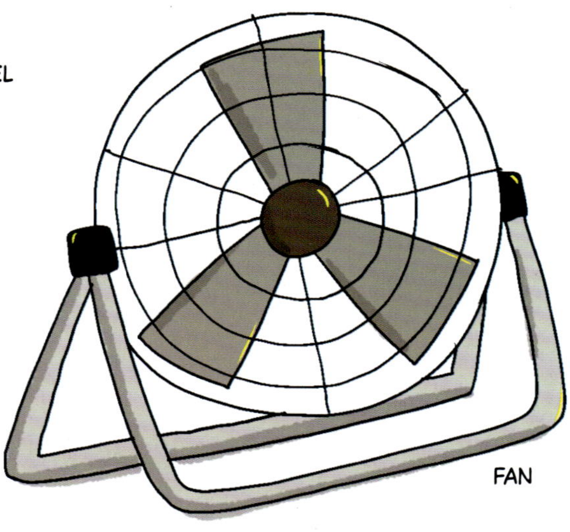
FAN

AND THEY'VE BEEN USED IN A HUGE VARIETY OF VEHICLES TOO...LIKE THIS ROMAN CHARIOT!

Trains, buses, and trolleys ...

And this – it's a unicycle!

Speedy motorbikes ...

Help!
And of course, roller skates! Oops!

Be careful!

POTTER'S WHEELS ARE WHEELS TOO! IN FACT, SOME EXPERTS THINK THEY WERE THE FIRST EVER WHEELS AND WERE INVENTED BEFORE ROLLING WHEELS.

CRAZY CATAPULTS

IN 1300S EUROPE, ENEMIES SOMETIMES ATTACKED EACH OTHER'S CASTLES ...
Prepare to attack!
... USING A CATAPULT-LIKE DEVICE CALLED A TREBUCHET.
Crumbly Castle will never be defeated!
Ha! We'll see ... I've got a new weapon!
Oh no – what's that!? Doesn't look good ...
FIRE!
Get ready ...
CRASH!
CRUNCH!
Help!

THEN ...
How would you like some cow dung next...
Yuck!
Eeeewwww!
Stinky!
THEN ...
Now launch me at the castle!
BUT ...
I've gone too far... arghhhh!!!
Goodbye! Have a nice trip!

PIVOT POWER

This is a trebuchet... a simple but deadly machine! It works using a basic machine called a lever, and you can try it yourself!

FIND A METAL OR WOODEN SPOON
BALANCE IT ON SOMETHING, LIKE AN ERASER.
PUT YOUR MISSILE HERE (NOT A ROCK! SOMETHING SOFT!)
DONK!
HIT DOWN ON THE HANDLE ...
Hey!
That's how a simple lever works!

WHAT IS A LEVER?

A LEVER IS JUST A RIGID STICK OR MACHINE PART THAT ROTATES AROUND A POINT.

.... THIS END GOES DOWN!
HERE'S THE LEVER
WHEN THIS END GOES UP ....
IT MOVES AROUND A POINT, CALLED THE PIVOT

THE TREBUCHET HAS A LEVER
THE HEAVY WEIGHT PULLS THIS END DOWN
MAKING THIS END ZOOM UP!

THE SPOON VERSION WORKS THE SAME WAY

A SEESAW IS A LEVER TOO!

EXTRA STRENGTH

LEVERS CAN GIVE YOU EXTRA POWER TO DO A TASK, LIKE LIFTING OR SQUASHING SOMETHING.

THIS LEVER HAS THE PIVOT POINT CLOSE TO ONE END
That means the other end moves farther – but this end moves with more force.
So I can use the lever to lift the proffessor!

THE FIRST TOILET

AT THE ROYAL COURT OF ENGLAND, IN THE 1580S ...
Harington, you may be my godson, but you tell too many rude jokes! Leave and do something useful!
Sorry, your majesty.
BACK IN HARINGTON'S HOUSE ...
I know what I can do! I'll invent a toilet that's better than this!
BEFORE FLUSHING TOILETS PEOPLE JUST USED A POT, LIKE THIS.
Look out!
Yuck! Do you mind!?
SO ...
The queen will love this!

WHEN THEY'D DONE THEIR BUSINESS, THEY HAD TO GET RID OF IT, SO THEY EMPTIED IT INTO THE STREET!

Ker-SPLOSH!
I present the "Ajax" flushing toilet! You sit here. When you've finished, you pull this handle. Water flows out of the cistern and washes everything away!*
TANK UNDERNEATH
OOH! Can you build one in the royal palace!?
*THEN A SERVANT EMPTIES OUT THE STINKY TANK LATER.
SO ...
It's ready, your majesty!
BUT...
Sadly, it didn't catch on. But one day, everyone will have one – I'm sure of it!

DOWN THE PAN

OF COURSE, WE'VE HAD TOILETS SINCE ANCIENT TIMES.

Like these Roman ones!

WATER FLOWED ALONG UNDERNEATH TO WASH THE WASTE AWAY.

PEOPLE HAVE ALSO USED CHAMBER POTS ...

CLOSE-STOOLS – WHICH WERE JUST CHAMBER POTS HIDDEN INSIDE A CHAIR

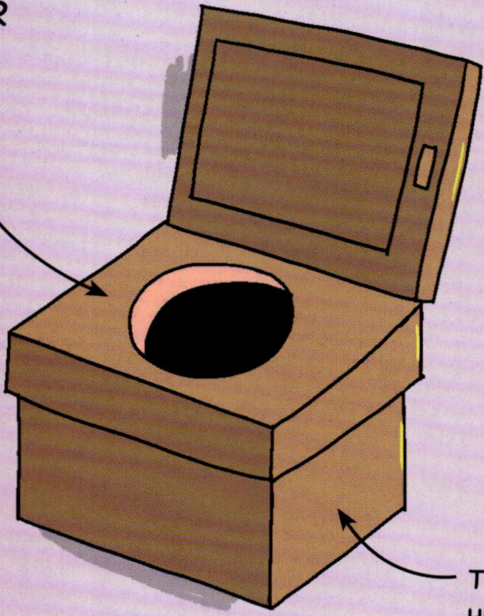

THE CHAMBER POT WAS HIDDEN IN HERE.

AND SCARY CASTLE TOILETS LIKE THESE!

THE TOILET WAS JUST A HOLE THAT LED OUT THROUGH THE CASTLE WALL.

TOILETS TODAY

AMAZINGLY, OVER 400 YEARS LATER, TOILETS STILL HAVE THE SAME BASIC DESIGN. IN SOME AREAS, THEY USE PLUMBING SYSTEMS, SO THEY FILL UP AND EMPTY AUTOMATICALLY.

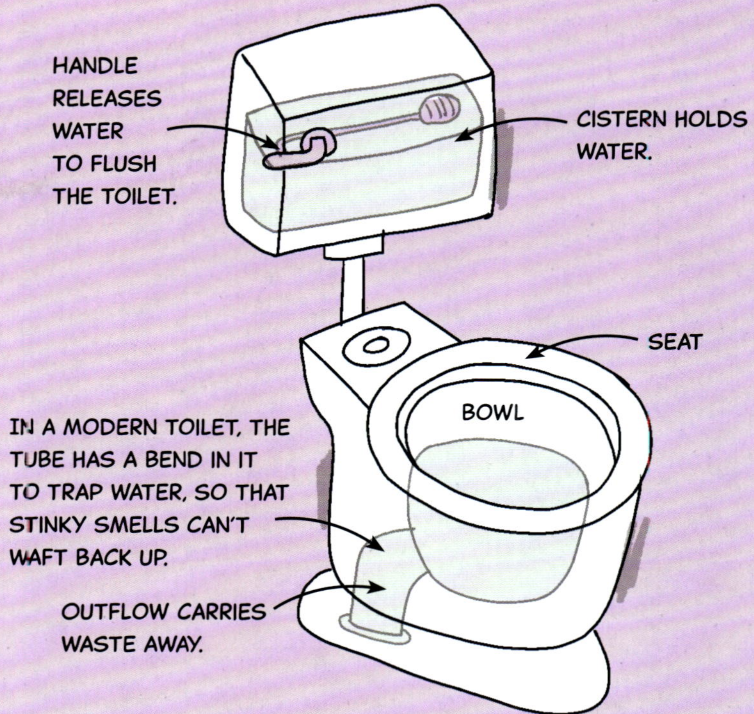

HANDLE RELEASES WATER TO FLUSH THE TOILET.
CISTERN HOLDS WATER.
SEAT
BOWL
IN A MODERN TOILET, THE TUBE HAS A BEND IN IT TO TRAP WATER, SO THAT STINKY SMELLS CAN'T WAFT BACK UP.
OUTFLOW CARRIES WASTE AWAY.

Wow! It's a computerized toilet!
Talking toilets like me are popular in Japan.
As well as talking, I lift the lid for you, heat the seat, play music, and flush myself!
That sounds a bit fancy to me!
I prefer my own toilet!

THE CASE OF THE SWALLOWED SPOON

AT THE HOSPITAL ...
Another busy day, looking inside people's insides!
X-RAY MACHINE
Ouch.
Hmm, looks like it's broken ...
I've got a bad stomachache.
Ooh, this is interesting! What's that in there?
It looks like a spoon ...
SO ...
That's a spoon in your stomach. You'll need surgery to get it out.
I don't remember swallowing that! How long will it take to remove?
Don't worry! It's quick and easy. A robot will do it!

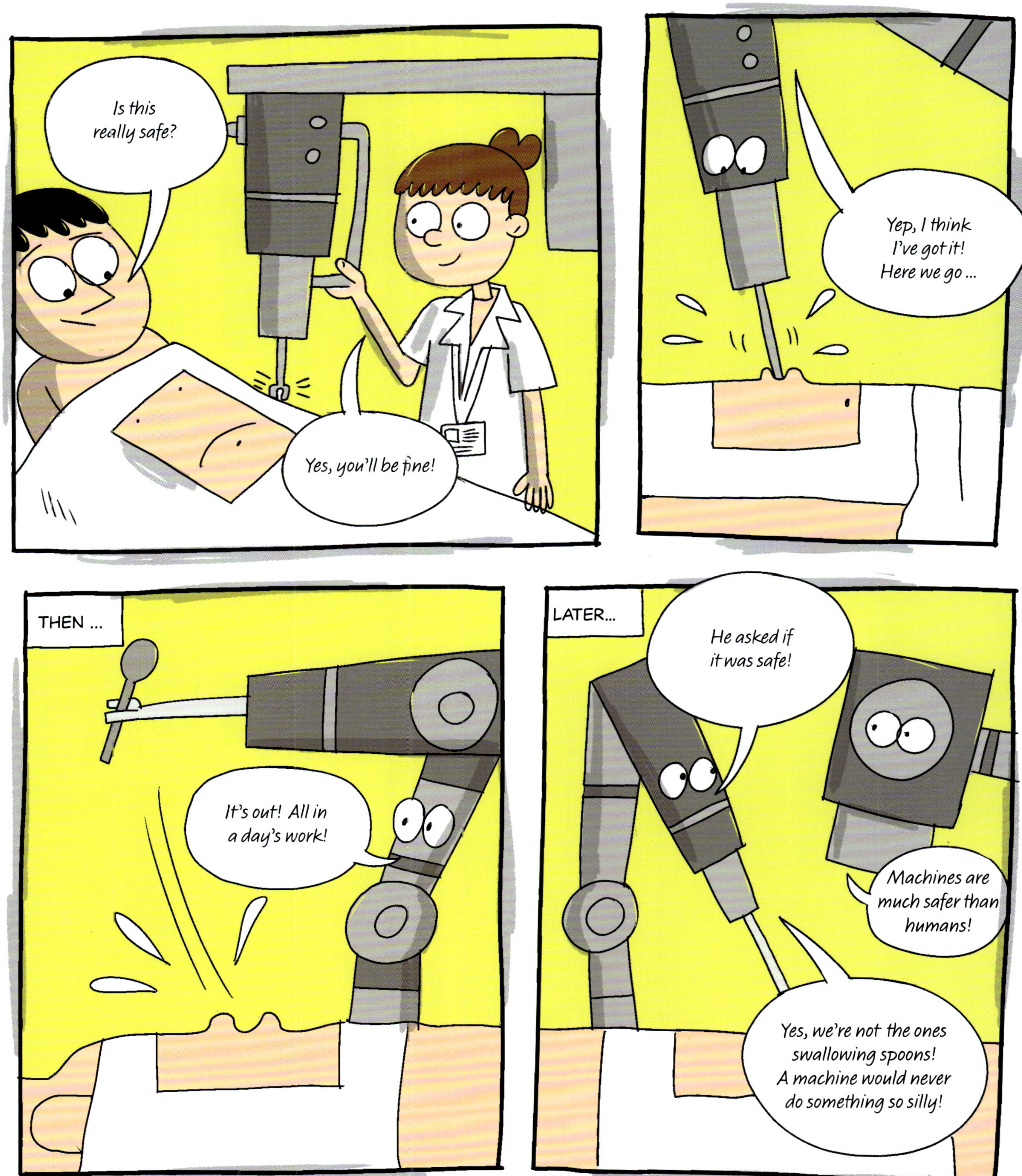
Is this really safe?
Yes, you'll be fine!
Yep, I think I've got it! Here we go ...
THEN ...
It's out! All in a day's work!
LATER...
He asked if it was safe!
Machines are much safer than humans!
Yes, we're not the ones swallowing spoons! A machine would never do something so silly!

MEDICAL MARVELS

Oh no! I've got a stomachache now! I hope it's not a spoon!
Oh good, I won't need an X-ray then!
I think you just had too much cake.
Huh? What are X-rays?

X-RAYS X-PLAINED!

X-RAYS ARE A KIND OF INVISIBLE LIGHT RAY. HUMANS CAN'T SEE THEM, BUT THEY CAN SHINE THROUGH SOME SOLID OBJECTS – INCLUDING OUR BODIES!

INSIDE THE MACHINE, A SPECIAL ELECTRIC CIRCUIT CREATES THE X-RAYS.
BONES (AND SPOONS!) BLOCK SOME OF THE RAYS, SO YOU CAN SEE THEM IN THE IMAGE.
I just zap X-ray waves at the patient, and they go right through! Then they're turned into a kind of photo, showing what's inside you.
THE TABLE UNDERNEATH THE PATIENT DETECTS THE X-RAYS.

LIFESAVING MACHINES

THE X-RAY MACHINE IS JUST ONE OF MANY BRILLIANT MEDICAL MACHINES. FOR EXAMPLE...

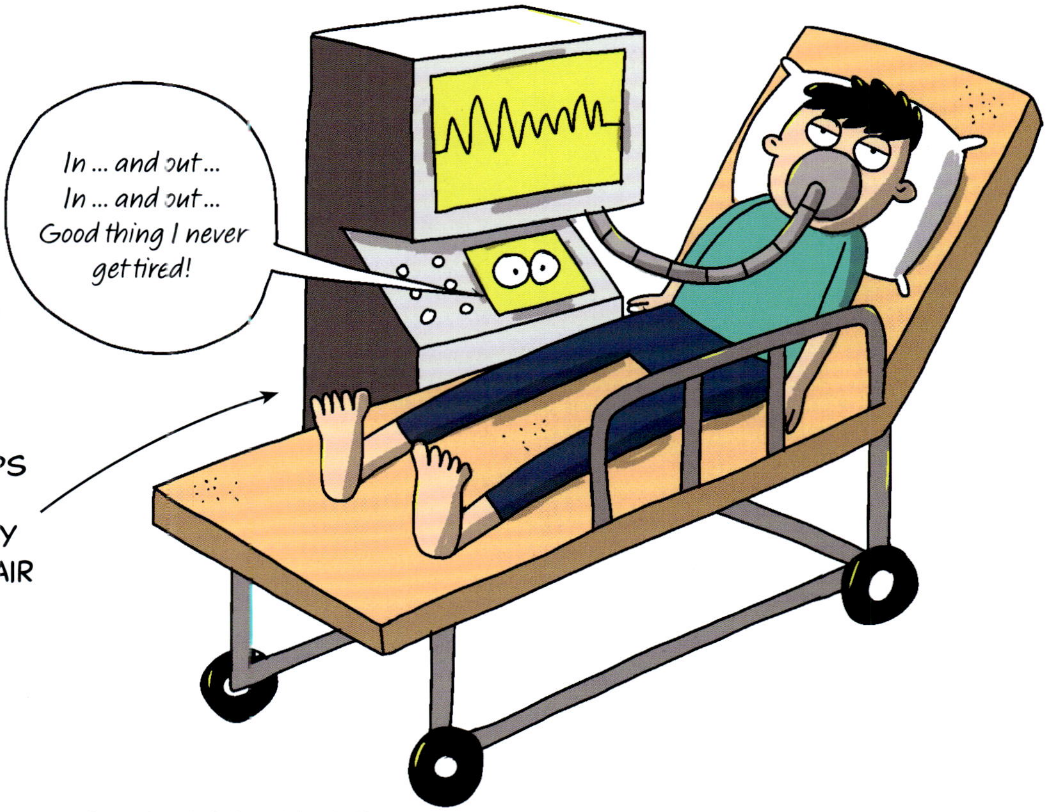
In ... and out...
In ... and out...
Good thing I never get tired!

A VENTILATOR HELPS PEOPLE BREATHE WHEN THEY'RE VERY SICK, BY PUSHING AIR INTO THEIR LUNGS.

AND ULTRASOUND MACHINES LOOK INSIDE YOU USING SOUND! THEY CAN DETECT ORGANS OR A BABY IN THE WOMB.

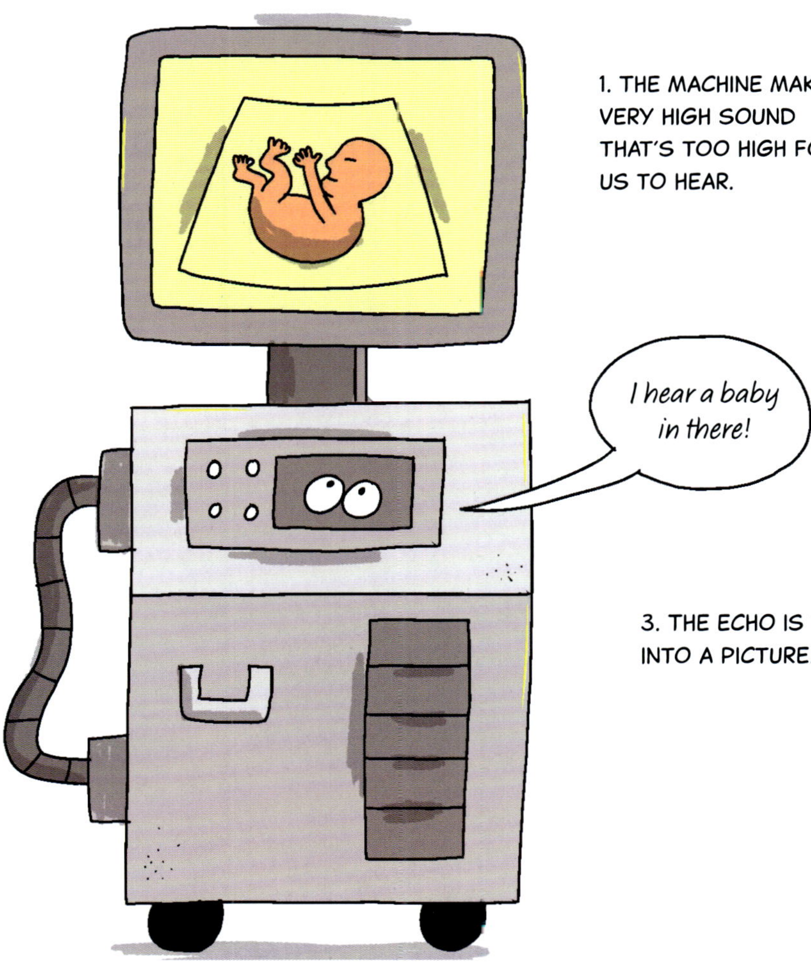
I hear a baby in there!

1. THE MACHINE MAKES VERY HIGH SOUND THAT'S TOO HIGH FOR US TO HEAR.

2. IT TRAVELS INTO THE BODY AND BOUNCES OFF THINGS, MAKING AN ECHO.

3. THE ECHO IS TURNED INTO A PICTURE.

DELIVERY DRONE MAYHEM

ONE DAY, NOT TOO FAR AWAY ...
Ok, all set to go!
DELIVERY DRONES ARE NOW BEING USED TO DELIVER EMERGENCY SUPPLIES, PACKAGES, AND EVEN TAKEOUT FOOD!
Woohoo! Up, up, and away!
Urgh, what's that!?
Oops, sorry!
THEN ...
Huh!? What are you doing up here!?
Just being a hoverboard!
STRANGE MACHINES MAY SOON FILL THE SKIES!
AND ...
Excuse me! I'm trying to land.
That was close! There's just too much going on up here!

Nearly there. Oh no! Now what!? What are they doing?
We're formation display drones! We're practicing for a big show tonight!
Very nice, but I have a delivery to make! Excuse me!
FINALLY...
I've arrived! This is the address!
Yay, my drone camera has arrived.
Oh no – even more drones!!!

FUTURISTIC FLYERS

When I was little, I thought that when I grew up, we'd all have jetpacks and flying cars! So where are they?

They're here! Check this out!

FLYING MACHINES

PEOPLE HAVE ALWAYS LONGED TO FLY LIKE BIRDS AND INSECTS CAN. WE'VE BEEN BUILDING FLYING MACHINES FOR HUNDREDS OF YEARS!

IT STARTED WITH HOT AIR BALLOONS, IN 1783.

We're flying!

THE FIRST POWERED PLANE FLEW IN 1903.

Hope I can figure out how to land!

AND SINCE THEN, WE'VE INVENTED LOTS MORE OF THEM ...

HELICOPER

3... 2... 1... We have lift-off!

SPACE ROCKET

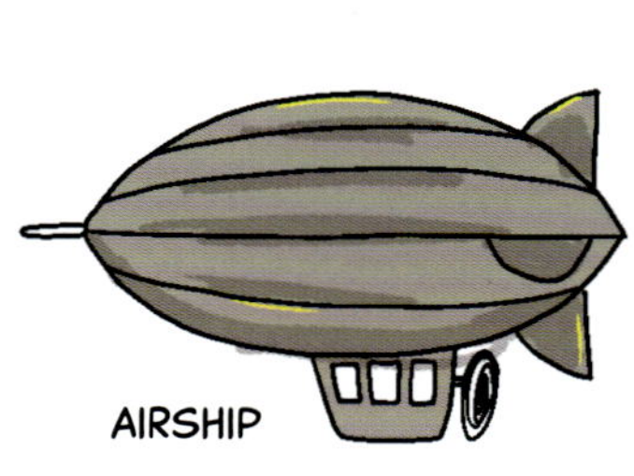

AIRSHIP

INTO THE FUTURE

MORE RECENTLY, WE'VE MADE FLYING MACHINES FROM SCI-FI MOVIES A REALITY ...

FITS ON YOUR BACK LIKE A BACKPACK
JET PACK
JET THRUSTERS

HOVERBOARD
A FLYING PLATFORM THAT YOU STAND ON

WINGSUIT
LIKE A TINY HUMAN PLANE!

DRONE REVOLUTION

DRONES ARE SMALL FLYING MACHINES THAT USE MINI-ROTORBLADES TO FLY. THEY'RE USED TO TAKE PHOTOS AND VIDEOS FROM THE AIR, TO CREATE LIT-UP DISPLAYS, AND TO DELIVER THINGS – AND THERE ARE ALSO NOW DRONE-POWERED FLYING CARS.

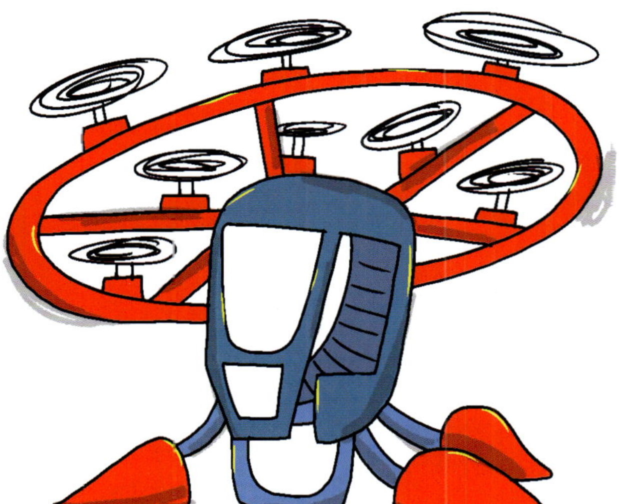

So why don't we all have our own?
They're still being developed – and they're very expensive!

GPS JOURNEYS TO THE SEA

ONE DAY, IN THE COUNTRYSIDE...
I'm ready for a lovely vacation!
And I'm not worried about getting lost...
... as my humans have installed a fancy new GPS!
Take the next left in 50 feet...
AND ...
Stay on this road for 5 miles.
This doesn't really seem like the quickest route. But it's very pretty!
THEN ...
Go straight ahead and continue for 3 miles.
Umm ... really?

BUT ...
Go straight ahead!
No! I'm not going in the sea! My engine will get wet!
Excuse me? Is there a road here, under the sea?
Of course not!
Don't be silly!
What's going on?
This doesn't seem right.
And the car's broken down!
We've gone totally the wrong way! We need to turn around!
Everyone has their bad days ...

MECHANICAL MISTAKES

Hmmm, how strange! How can a machine get something so wrong?
I thought GPS was supposed to be better than old-fashioned maps!

HOW GPS WORKS

GPS WORKS BECAUSE OF SATELLITES – A KIND OF SPACECRAFT THAT ORBITS THE PLANET. GPS INSTRUCTIONS SEND SIGNALS TO SATELLITES. THE SATELLITES CALCULATE EXACTLY WHERE THE GPS USER IS AND SENDS SIGNALS BACK, SO THE GPS CAN PLAN A ROUTE USING MAPS.

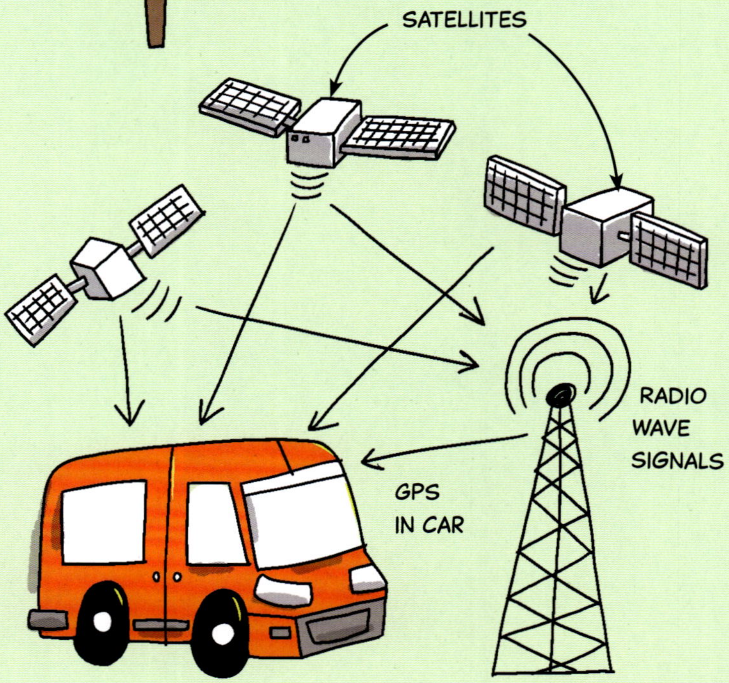
SATELLITES
RADIO WAVE SIGNALS
GPS IN CAR

It's not MY fault! You humans programmed me!
It should work perfectly, but sometimes, GPS sends people the wrong way!

MACHINES IN CONTROL

IN THE MODERN WORLD, WE USE A LOT OF MACHINES, AND WE OFTEN PUT OUR TRUST IN THEM.

GPS TELL US WHERE TO GO.

Which way next?

COMPUTERIZED MACHINES IN SHOPS AND BANKS CONTROL OUR MONEY.

BANK
PAY
Beep! You have paid

AUTOMATED TRAFFIC LIGHTS STOP VEHICLES FROM CRASHING.

Stop! Let people cross.

IF MACHINES LIKE THESE GO WRONG, IT CAN CAUSE BIG PROBLEMS!

WE'RE IN CHARGE

MACHINES ARE USEFUL, BUT WE STILL NEED TO USE COMMON SENSE, AND NOT DO WHATEVER THEY TELL US!

CAT FOOD
Oh no – the internet's not working! I can't order cat food.
Or I can just go to the store ...
What!? I'll starve!

WHICH BIKE IS BEST?

THE GREAT BIKE RACE IS ABOUT TO BEGIN. OUR THREE CONTENDERS ARE...
IN LANE 1, IT'S THE FIRST EVER PEDAL BIKE!
The original and best!
I was invented in 1839 by Kirkpatrick Macmillan.
THE PEDALS MOVED FORWARD AND BACKWARD, AND WERE ATTACHED TO THE BACK WHEEL WITH RODS.
IN LANE 2, IT'S THE CLASSIC PEDAL BIKE!
This trusted bike has been used by cyclists everywhere since the 1880s – and it's still going strong!
Can't beat a trusty pedal bike!
ON THIS BIKE, THE PEDALS GO ROUND AND ROUND. A CHAIN LINKS THEM TO THE BACK WHEEL, MAKING IT TURN.
IN LANE 3, IT'S THE HIGH-TECH E-BIKE!
I can just sit back and let the bike do the work!
E-bikes rule!
THIS BIKE USES BATTERIES SO YOU DON'T HAVE TO PEDAL MUCH!

Ready, set, go!
Eat dirt, losers!
BUT...
Oh no – my battery ran out!
And e-bikes are really heavy to pedal!
THEN ...
CRASH
PYOINNGG!
Oh no! My chain's come off!
SO ...
Heh heh! Slow and steady wins the race!

PEDAL POWER

MACMILLAN'S TREADLE BIKE WAS THE FIRST PEDAL-POWERED CYCLE, AND IT WASN'T VERY HIGH-TECH. BUT SIMPLER MACHINES HAVE FEWER PARTS THAT CAN GO WRONG.

A MODERN PEDAL BIKE'S CHAINS AND GEARS MAKE IT MORE EFFICIENT, BUT THEY CAN BREAK.

AND E-BIKES ARE GREAT WHEN YOU NEED SOME EXTRA POWER – BUT THE BATTERY NEEDS RECHARGING!

So which bike is best? They all have different advantages ...

PEDAL REVOLUTION

BUT WHATEVER TYPE OF BIKE YOU RIDE, IT'S AN AMAZINGLY USEFUL AND GREEN INVENTION!

Bikes are cheaper than cars ...
... they can whizz past traffic jams ...
TRICYCLE
RICKSHAW

ROUND AND ROUND AND ROUND AND ROUND ...

PEDALS ARE ONE OF MANY INVENTIONS BASED ON THE WHEEL (SEE PAGE 8).

1. THE PEDALS ARE ATTACHED TO A CRANK, OR AXLE.

2. YOU PUSH THEM AROUND WITH YOUR FEET.

3. AND A CHAIN OR OTHER PART TRANSFERS THE SPINNING MOVEMENT TO WHERE IT'S NEEDED.

HUMAN-POWERED PEDAL PLANE
... provide great exercise ...
PADDLEBOAT
... and don't pollute the planet!
Pedals can be used to power lots of things, such as all the things in this picture !

MOUSE VS MOUSE

IN AN OFFICE, LATE ONE NIGHT...
The coast is clear! Time to find some food ...
Sniffle, sniffle ... any crumbs up here?
Uh!? What's that!?
What do you mean, "What's that?" I'm a mouse, of course!
No, you're not! I'm a mouse! You don't look like a mouse to me ...
I'm a computer mouse! Humans use me to move a pointer on the computer screen. I'm very useful! And I have a tail, just like you.
Real mice run around looking for crumbs and giving humans a fright. You're nothing like a mouse!
And that's not a tail. It's a wire!
Whatever!
Anyway ... did you just say CRUMBS?

Yes, have you seen any? I LOVE crumbs.
I hate crumbs! My human ALWAYS eats snacks and drop crumbs everywhere! Look over here!
Well, if you want those crumbs cleaned up, I'm your mouse!
Be my guest!
NIBBLE
CRUNCH
Mmmmm! These are good crumbs!
Finally, a nice, clean, tidy desk! Can you come back tomorrow night?

COMPUTER CONTROL

Well, it looks a bit like a real mouse!
But not that much!

A COMPUTER MOUSE NEEDS TO BE CONNECTED TO A COMPUTER TO WORK. IT LETS YOU CONTROL THE MOVEMENTS OF THE LITTLE ARROW CURSOR ON THE SCREEN AND SELECT ACTIONS.

POINTING MACHINE

WHEN THE COMPUTER MOUSE WAS FIRST INVENTED IN 1964, IT WAS CALLED THE "X-Y POSITION INDICATOR." BUT BEFORE LONG ...

I think I'll just call it a mouse for short.

HOW DOES IT WORK?

A MOUSE IS LINKED TO A COMPUTER BY A WIRE OR BY WIRELESS SIGNALS. AS YOU MOVE THE MOUSE AROUND, IT SENSES THE MOVEMENT ACROSS THE DESK AND SENDS SIGNALS TO THE COMPUTER TO MOVE A POINTER ON THE SCREEN.

YOU PRESS A BUTTON ON THE MOUSE TO "CLICK" ON SOMETHING.

Before the mouse, you had to type instructions into the computer to do anything! Today, we have many more mouse-like inventions too. My laptop has a touchpad instead.

You can play video games with a special controller or a joystick.

And smartphones and tablets have touchscreens!

COMPUTER WORLD

THE MOUSE IS JUST A SMALL PART OF THE COMPUTER TECHNOLOGY THAT'S ALL AROUND US IN THE MODERN WORLD.

12
58
NAV

There are computers and electronic machines everywhere!

ROBODOG TO THE RESCUE!

ON A REMOTE MOUNTAINSIDE...
I'm totally lost! My phone is out of power, I don't know where I am, and it's getting dark!
THAT NIGHT...
CREAK
WHIRR
Wh-what's that?
THEN ...
Aaargh! A weird robot creature. Get away from me!
BEEP! ZZZZZZT! Target located!
AND...
Help!
Stop! My mission is to rescue you! I am the RoboDog-2000 mountain rescue bot!

BUT...
I'm rescuing you, silly human! I have some emergency supplies.
Please don't hurt me!
What are you?
I told you! I'm a robot rescue dog!
SO...
RoboDog-2000 calling rescue team! Human target located! Send help!
SO...
Phew! Someone's here to rescue me at last! Save me from this scary robot!

ROBOT WORLD

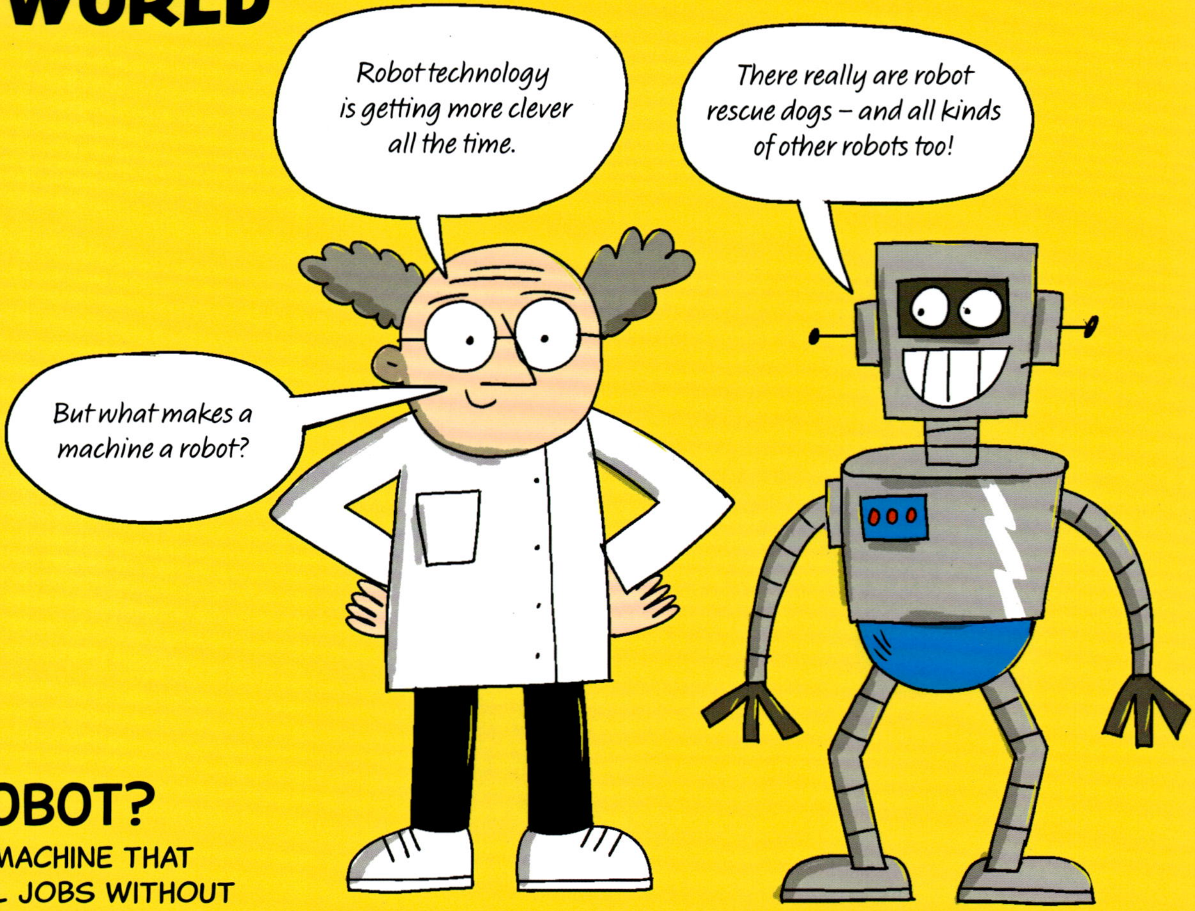
Robot technology is getting more clever all the time.
There really are robot rescue dogs – and all kinds of other robots too!
But what makes a machine a robot?

IS IT A ROBOT?

A ROBOT IS A MACHINE THAT CAN DO USEFUL JOBS WITHOUT A HUMAN CONTROLLING IT. SOME CAN SENSE THEIR SURROUNDINGS, LEARN, AND MAKE DECISIONS TOO.

MOST ROBOTS HAVE A MACHINE BODY AND A COMPUTER WITH SOFTWARE THAT TELLS THEM HOW TO DO THINGS.

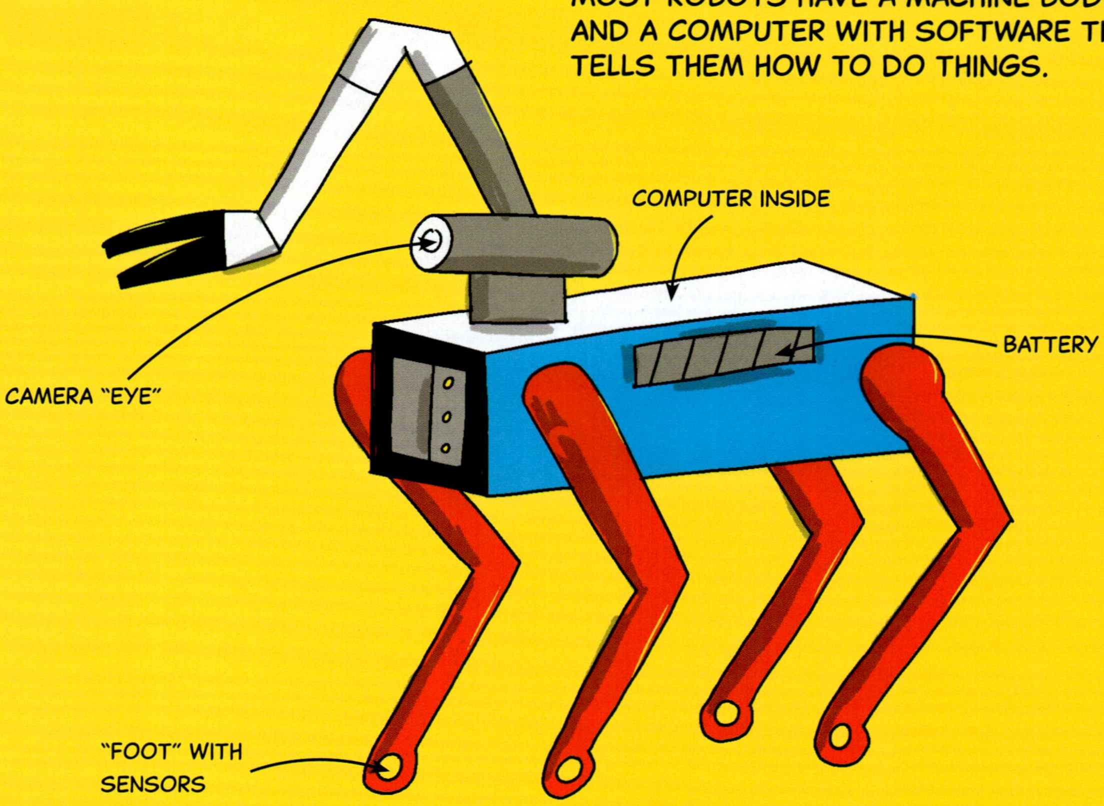
COMPUTER INSIDE
BATTERY
CAMERA "EYE"
"FOOT" WITH SENSORS

MEET THE ROBOTS

ROBOTS COME IN MANY SHAPES AND SIZES.
AND WHAT THEY CAN DO IS CONSTANTLY EVOLVING – FROM TALKING TO DANCING OR PLAYING SPORTS!

When people think of a robot, they often imagine a human-shaped or "humanoid" robot – just like me!
Pleased to meet you ...

Whee ...

SOME ROBOTS ARE BUILT TO DO A PARTICULAR JOB, LIKE THIS FACTORY ROBOT.

I'll just stick this bit in – you're almost finished!
Thanks!

AND LOTS OF ROBOTS ARE INSPIRED BY ANIMALS, LIKE THESE:

SCI-FI FOGBOTS

SOMEWHERE IN A SUPERVILLAIN'S SECRET LAIR...
After years of work, my new invention is ready. Meet the fogbots!
They can work together to make any object or machine I want!
Your wish is our command!
OK, make me a flying carpet with a coffee machine.
Coffee
No problem!
Now make a city-destroying giant monster robot!
We're on it!

With my fogbots, I'll soon be able to take over the world! Mwah-ha-ha-ha-ha-ha-ha!
Excuse me! This is a science book, not science fiction! Robots like these don't really exist!
Oh alright, spoilsport! They don't exist YET!
But they will eventually! Robots keep getting smaller and smarter – so it's only a matter of time ...
And then I will definitely TAKE OVER THE WORLD! Mwah-ha-ha-ha-ha-ha-ha ...

COULD THIS REALLY HAPPEN? TURN THE PAGE TO FIND OUT ...

TINY TECHNOLOGY

ROBOTS REALLY CAN BE TINY. IN FACT, SCIENTISTS HAVE MADE SOME ROBOTS AND OTHER MACHINES SO SMALL THAT WE NEED A TOOL CALLED A MICROSCOPE TO SEE THEM!

It's an area of science called nanotechnology. Nano means tiny!

NANOCARS

FOR EXAMPLE, THEY'VE MADE TINY INVISIBLE CARS THAT CAN REALLY MOVE!

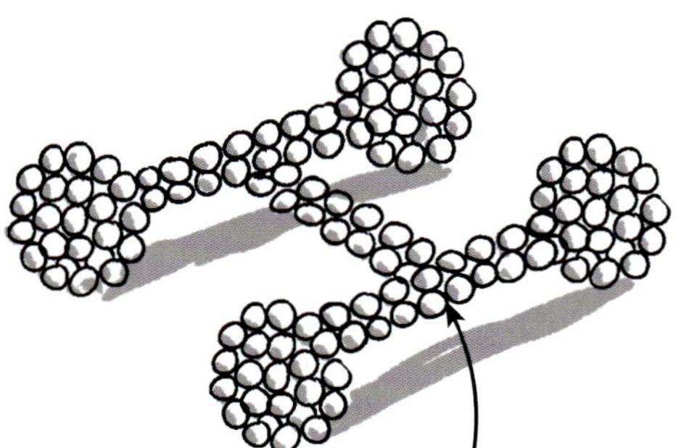

THEY LOOK LIKE THIS BUT A LOT SMALLER

You need to look very carefully. And don't step on it!
VROOM!

Where is it?

MACHINES MAKE MACHINES

BUT WHAT ABOUT SWARMS OF TINY ROBOTS THAT CAN ARRANGE THEMSELVES INTO ANY SHAPE AND FORM BIGGER MACHINES OR ROBOTS? THEY'RE FEATURED IN SCI-FI MOVIES ....

But could it come true?
Maybe!

SCIENTISTS REALLY ARE WORKING ON ROBOTS LIKE THIS. THEY'RE KNOWN AS UTILITY FOG, OR "FOGLETS." HOWEVER, THEY'RE NOT QUITE READY YET! SO FAR, THEY CAN ONLY FORM SIMPLE SHAPES, USUALLY ON A FLAT SURFACE.

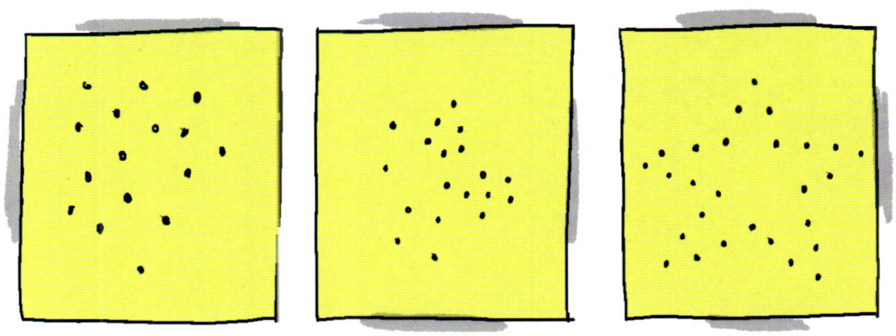

AND THERE'S ANOTHER PROBLEM ...

It's very hard to give a small robot like this enough energy to move around and build working objects.
It might work ... one day!
My battery's out!

GLOSSARY

CATAPULT A MACHINE OR SMALL DEVICE THAT SHOOTS A MISSILE.

CISTERN A WATER TANK, ESPECIALLY THE TYPE THAT PROVIDES WATER TO FLUSH A TOILET.

DRONE A SMALL, REMOTE-CONTROLLED OR AUTOMATIC FLYING MACHINE.

ECHO SOUND THAT BOUNCES OFF A SURFACE AND RETURNS BACK THE WAY IT CAME.

FOGLETS TINY ROBOTS THAT CAN JOIN TOGETHER TO CREATE LARGER OBJECTS.

JETPACK A FLYING MACHINE THAT IS WORN LIKE A BACKPACK AND USES JET THRUSTERS TO FLY.

LEVER A RIGID BAR OR POLE THAT RESTS ON A POINT OR PIVOT, AND WORKS LIKE A SEESAW.

MOUSE IN TECHNOLOGY, A DEVICE USED TO MOVE A POINTER AROUND ON A COMPUTER SCREEN.

NANOTECHNOLOGY MAKING MACHINES AND OTHER TECHNOLOGY ON A MICROSCOPICALLY TINY SCALE.

PIVOT A POINT OR SUPPORTING PART THAT A LEVER OR OTHER DEVICE BALANCES OR ROTATES ON.

ROBOT A MACHINE THAT CAN DO COMPLEX TASKS AND ACTIONS ON ITS OWN, USUALLY PROGRAMMED BY A COMPUTER.

SATELLITE AN OBJECT THAT ORBITS AROUND EARTH, OR AROUND ANOTHER OBJECT IN SPACE.

TECHNOLOGY MACHINES, GADGETS, AND INVENTIONS MADE TO DO USEFUL JOBS.

TOUCHPAD A PAD ON A COMPUTER THAT SENSES TOUCH AND CAN BE USED TO MOVE A POINTER ON THE SCREEN.

TOUCHSCREEN A SCREEN ON A PHONE, TABLET, OR OTHER COMPUTER THAT SENSES TOUCH AND CAN BE USED TO CONTROL THE DEVICE.

TREADLE A KIND OF LEVER MOVED BY THE FEET, USED TO POWER A MACHINE.

ULTRASOUND VERY HIGH-PITCHED SOUND THAT HUMANS CAN'T HEAR.

UTILITY FOG A FUTURISTIC IDEA FOR A CLOUD OF TINY "FOGLET" ROBOTS THAT COULD CHANGE SHAPE TO MAKE ANY OBJECT OR MACHINE.

X-RAY A KIND OF ENERGY RAY THAT CAN PASS THROUGH PARTS OF THE BODY, USED TO MAKE PHOTOS OF OUR INSIDES.

QUIZ

1. WHICH OF THESE INVENTIONS DOES NOT CONTAIN A WHEEL?

A. A WINDMILL

B. A RECORD PLAYER

C. A CHAMBER POT

2. WHAT WERE TREBUCHETS USED FOR?

A. MOVING STONE BUILDING BLOCKS

B. SHOOTING MISSILES AT CASTLES

C. SAILING ACROSS OCEANS

3. WHO DID JOHN HARINGTON MAKE A TOILET FOR?

A. QUEEN ELIZABETH I

B. QUEEN CLEOPATRA

C. QUEEN VICTORIA

4. WHAT KIND OF RAYS CAN TAKE A PHOTO OF YOUR INSIDES?

A. X-RAYS

B. Y-RAYS

C. Z-RAYS

5. WHICH OF THESE FLYING MACHINES CAME FIRST?

A. PLANE

B. HOT AIR BALLOON

C. JETPACK

6. WHICH OF THESE THINGS CAN ORBIT THE EARTH?

A. SATELLITES

B. SATURN

C. THE SUN

7. WHAT LINKS A BIKE'S PEDALS TO ITS BACK WHEEL TO MAKE IT TURN?

A. AN ELASTIC BAND

B. A ROPE

C. A CHAIN

8. WHAT IS AN "X-Y POSITION INDICATOR" NOW CALLED?

A. A RAT

B. A MOUSE

C. A SQUIRREL

9. WILL ROBOTS TAKE OVER THE WORLD?

A. YES

B. NO

C. NO ONE IS SURE YET

10. WHAT DO YOU CALL A CAR THAT'S SO SMALL YOU CAN'T SEE IT?

A. A NONOCAR

B. A NANOCAR

C. A NANACAR

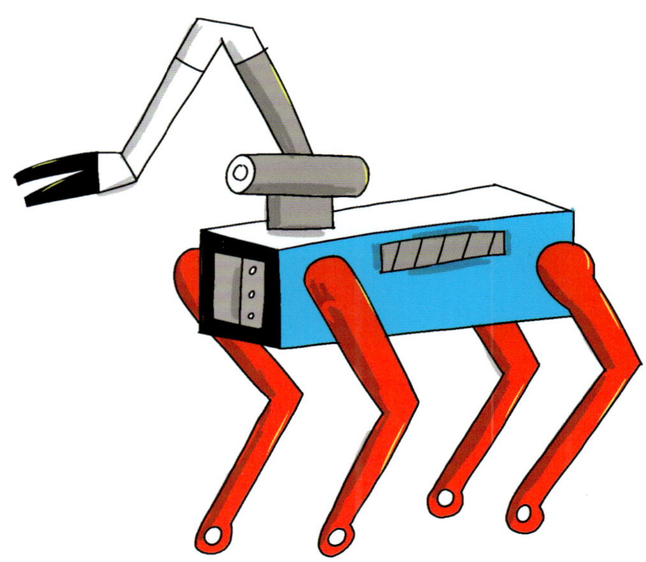

ANSWERS: 1. C 2. B 3. A 4. A 5. B 6. A 7. C 8. B 9. C 10. B

INDEX

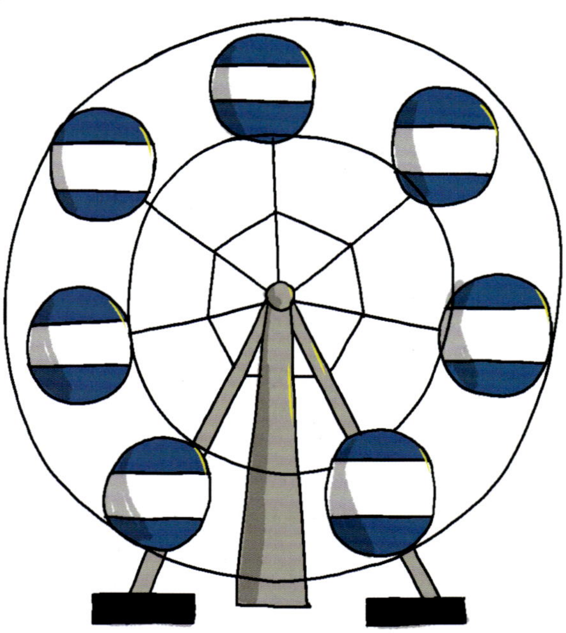